Summary of

The 4 Disciplines of Execution

Achieving Your Wildly Important Goals

by Chris McChesney, Sean Covey, and Jim Huling

Instaread

Please Note

This is a summary with analysis.

Table of Contents

Overview

The 4 Disciplines of Execution is a guide for businesses to reliably commit to the goals and plans they set, authored by associates from FranklinCovey, a management consultancy. Rather than focusing on what a business must accomplish to be successful, the four disciplines establish how to accomplish those things.

One reason commitments tend to be abandoned in business is that new projects and goals are less urgent than the day-to-day tasks of each individual employee, which the authors call the "whirlwind." The key to commitment fulfillment is for new tasks to take up only a small portion of each employee's time, but for that employee to be held accountable for completing them.

The first discipline is to settle on one or two wildly important goals (WIGs). These are the things that would have the most significant impact on progress toward the business's long-term goals. In the second discipline, the WIG is broken down into a few leading indicators that can predict whether the WIG will be accomplished. The indicators must be things that are directly affected by the employees. The third discipline is creating a highly visible, quickly understood scoreboard that displays progress toward the WIG and the leading indicators. The final discipline is a brief weekly meeting where every employee updates the team on his or her individual accomplishments toward the WIG and leading indicators, followed by discussions about what each person must commit to doing in the coming week.

Implementing the four disciplines in a business is a process that depends on consistency, focus, strong leadership, and accountability. Even employees who resist the new measures at first will tend to adopt them willingly over time. Once the WIGs and lead measures have been clearly defined for each team, a company must train leaders on how to enforce the disciplines. Then they can launch the disciplines, carry out the plan with regular coaching, and assess progress on a quarterly basis. Many of FranklinCovey's clients have used the four disciplines of execution to implement their programs and achieve their goals.

Important People

Chris McChesney leads design and development of principles of execution at consultancy FranklinCovey.

Sean Covey oversees global solutions and operations for FranklinCovey, where he is the chief product architect. He is the son of self-help author Stephen Covey.

Jim Huling is the managing consultant of the four disciplines of execution at FranklinCovey. He was previously the chief information officer at Experian and the chief executive officer at Matrix Resources before he founded his own consultancy.

Stephen Covey (1932-2012) was the author of a variety of self-help books including *The 7 Habits of Highly Effective People* (1989).

Scott Thele leads the execution practice at FranklinCovey.

Beverly J. Walker was the commissioner of the Georgia Department of Human Services and the deputy chief of staff for the City of Chicago. She later became a consultant with FranklinCovey and is now a director of public sector practice for Deloitte Consulting.

Key Takeaways

1. The chief obstacle to sustaining progress toward goals in a business is the whirlwind of everyday activity that is more urgent but less important.

2. The first discipline needed to pursue an important goal is to narrow the list of goals down to the one or two most wildly important. It is expressed as an action with a starting point, end goal, and time frame.

3. A good wildly important goal (WIG) has a high impact and is defined with input from both leaders and team members. It is measurable and directly impacted by the team and its leader.

4. The second discipline of execution is defining the lead measures that employees can affect and that will predict progress toward the wildly important goal.

5. Lead measures are either specific behaviors by employees or the outcomes of those behaviors, but regardless they must be high-impact, ongoing processes.

6. The third discipline of execution is creating a simple and comprehensible scoreboard that shows employees' progress toward the wildly important goal and the lead measures relative to the projected progress needed to succeed.

7. It is important for employees themselves to keep score and to celebrate when they win. Someone must be responsible for keeping the scoreboard up to date.

8. The fourth discipline of execution is to schedule regular weekly meetings that hold employees accountable for their progress on the lead measures and encourage them to make their own commitments for the coming week.

9. Implementing the four disciplines is a process for the whole team but is driven by the leader. It requires six steps, from clearly defining the WIG and lead measures to training leaders, launching the initiative, constant coaching, and quarterly updates.

10. Common obstacles to implementation can be avoided with consistency, accountability, and focus enforced by the leader.

Thank you for purchasing this Instaread book

**Download the Instaread mobile app to get
unlimited text & audio summaries
of bestselling books.**

Visit Instaread.co
to learn more.

Analysis

Key Takeaway 1

The chief obstacle to sustaining progress toward goals in a business is the whirlwind of everyday activity that is more urgent but less important.

Analysis

Many special projects in business do not last long enough for their goals to be accomplished because execution is more challenging than making a plan. The whirlwind of daily activity can bury special tasks, which are not as urgent even if they are important. Instead of developing programs to manage the whirlwind or switch it for special project execution, the best strategy is to find ways to make new projects take a small amount of time so that the whirlwind tasks can still be accomplished.

The whirlwind can include tasks that are introduced from the company's existing inefficiencies or because of economic challenges, as pharmaceutical company Banner discovered just before it implemented the four disciplines. Among the fire-fighting tasks it had to manage were negative business results, delivery that was on time only 53 percent of the time, work that had to be redone 146 times in a single year, and material losses equivalent to 4.1 percent of revenue. The execution quotient test, a FranklinCovey product that measures execution weaknesses, revealed that Banner also had low levels of trust within the organization, little collaboration, and insufficient accountability in teams. [1] While the four disciplines are not designed to completely eliminate the whirlwind of tasks stemming from problems like these, it takes away only a small amount of time from the whirlwind tasks while gradually reducing the need for re-work.

Key Takeaway 2

The first discipline needed to pursue an important goal is to narrow the list of goals down to the one or two most wildly important. It is expressed as an action with a starting point, end goal, and time frame.

Analysis

A wildly important goal is phrased as going from "X" to "Y" by "when." It is important to have only one, or two at most, because having more than that means that energies will be divided and individual goals are less likely to be completed. While some companies have a large number of goals they would like to accomplish, there is usually one with the most impact that the employees are most likely to affect.

Narrowing commitments to the fewest possible tasks or goals is a popular topic in the self-help genre. In *The One Thing* (2013), Gary Keller writes that successful people are the ones who narrow their energies to very few tasks with the most impact. Focusing on those tasks ensures that energy is most efficiently applied, which makes that person seem disproportionately productive. Similar to the advice of the four disciplines, Keller recommends turning down the goals that are appealing and would be good to accomplish, but which are not the most important at that moment. [2] Other popular self-help books, such as Marie Kondo's *The Life-Changing Magic of Tidying*

Up (2014), advocate minimizing possessions and clutter. Some advocate for simplified diets, such as *The Simplified Diet* by James Anderson (2011), or for relaxing the rules for success, such as Brené Brown's *The Gifts of Imperfection* (2010). The four disciplines promise not to increase stress because they do not take much time from the tasks that make up the whirlwind.

Key Takeaway 3

A good wildly important goal (WIG) has a high impact and is defined with input from both leaders and team members. It is measurable and directly impacted by the team and its leader.

Analysis

Implementing a WIG involves input from the entire team. Individual departments within an organization might have their own WIGs, but the department WIG must be aligned with that of the company. Having a unique WIG can give a team more impact on the result than if they pursued the company WIG, so they can be more invested while also improving chances that the company will accomplish its goal.

For example, FranklinCovey consulted for an unnamed US agency working in package delivery. The agency faced considerable challenges due to economic difficulties and organizational weaknesses in customer service outlets. The district leaders for the customer service outlets decided to implement the four disciplines of execution. The team of leaders used a set of long-term success factors from the CEO's goals to find four key areas where effort would be best applied, then used those to identify WIGs that they could track in their specific district. Within the areas of employee satisfaction, product operations, retail operations, and customer service, the WIGs were customized for the particular district to which they were applied. The team leader also appointed a single leader for each **WIG** to ensure that each one was applied and tracked in the best way across every team and outlet. [3]

Key Takeaway 4

The second discipline of execution is defining the lead measures that employees can affect and that will predict progress toward the wildly important goal.

Analysis

Most company indicators are lagging measures because they indicate the company's previous performance. Leading indicators, on the other hand, measure behaviors or factors that can predict lagging indicator performance and which the company's employees can impact directly.

Leading indicators are so important in safety programs in construction that they are increasingly becoming the industry standard. Construction companies have not only implemented leading measures as part of the four disciplines of execution, but also as part of standards that could eventually become guidelines promoted by the Occupational Safety and Health Administration in the United States. [4] These indicators, often connected with data to decreased injuries and fewer near-miss incidents, include measuring attendance and frequency of morning meetings. If the wildly important goal is the lagging indicator of decreased frequency of injuries, a leading indicator that workers can influence and which can be used to predict injuries is attendance at these kinds of meetings.

Key Takeaway 5

Lead measures are either specific behaviors by employees or the outcomes of those behaviors, but regardless they must be high-impact, ongoing processes.

Analysis

Lead measures come in two forms. Small outcomes display a short-term result that can be measured by impacts, like out-of-stock items. Leveraged behaviors track a particular behavior, like letters sent or calls made. These lead measures follow the same implementation steps as the WIG itself and must be the most high-impact indicators. As employees work to improve the lead indicators, the lagging indicator will improve over time.

As this applies to an example in personal life, like learning how to speak a language, a small outcome indicator would be something like the ability to translate words on flashcards. A leveraged behavior indicator in the same context is minutes spent reading and conversing in the language. If individuals have the WIG of being able to hold a simple conversation in the target language within three months, they might plan both of those lead indicators with the goal of memorization of a stack of 20 new vocabulary words each day and 30 minutes of reading or speaking in the language every day. These leading indicators are directly impacted by regular practice and commitment, and they are key to increasing capability with a new language. They are also easy to measure.

Key Takeaway 6

The third discipline of execution is creating a simple and comprehensible scoreboard that shows employees' progress toward the wildly important goal and the lead measures relative to the projected progress needed to succeed.

Analysis

Employee engagement increases when employees are keeping score and view projects as a competition. Unlike conventional dashboards of data maintained by executives to track progress toward a goal, which often include a lot of data that can be used to seek reasons for certain trends, a scoreboard should track only a few goals in a simple, visual format that also displays how progress compares to that required to achieve the goal.

As the manager of a steel mill in the 1900s, Charles Schwab created an extremely simple and motivating scoreboard to encourage competition between the day and night shifts. He wrote the number of heats the day shift completed in chalk on the floor, "6," and left it for the night shift to see. In the morning, the night shift had erased the 6 and written "7" in its place for the number of heats they completed. In response, the day shift worked extra hard and were able to write "10" on the floor at the end of their shift. Eventually, the mill was producing more steel than others in the same plant. [5] The chalk numbers were easy to understand, the employees updated them regularly to celebrate their successes, and they reflected numbers that the employees themselves could impact.

Key Takeaway 7

It is important for employees themselves to keep score and to celebrate when they win. Someone must be responsible for keeping the scoreboard up to date.

Analysis

Each week, employees must present to each other what they did to advance the lead measures and WIG. They also must make commitments for the coming week, meaning that each week's agenda is planned to adapt to challenges as they arise. Regular meetings ensure that employees hold each other accountable.

The scoreboard should be updated regularly by a team member to ensure that everyone can tell right away whether the team is succeeding. Scoreboards without accountability will be abandoned over time and cease to motivate the team. Strong teams that are motivated by their scoreboards will celebrate victories along the way.

The latest in data analysis and visualization technology makes these scoreboards easier to implement than ever before. Many data visualization platforms give users the ability to connect to an actively updated data source, so that if individuals update their lead measures through a shared data file, a connected visualization dashboard hosted on an accessible network intranet page could display the progress on the scoreboard in real time. If employees consistently record their progress and refer to the scoreboard whenever they have their weekly WIG sessions, the scoreboard can display the data in different ways with just a few clicks. They can adjust their goals to be more ambitious if the team agrees that it needs a greater challenge. A dynamic display can also automatically detect when the team has reached a goal and alert them that it is time to celebrate. Or, if the team fails to reach its goals, it might automatically adjust to display the amount of progress that would be needed to keep them on track, all without giving in to human biases that might exaggerate progress or soften failure to save emotions.

Key Takeaway 8

The fourth discipline of execution is to schedule regular weekly meetings that hold employees accountable for their progress on the lead measures and encourage them to make their own commitments for the coming week.

Analysis

The weekly sessions create a cadence of accountability and take up very little time in team members' schedule. They are predictable because they always cover the same three subjects. In WIG sessions, team members are encouraged to help by clearing paths through barriers for each other. They are also opportunities to celebrate victories and discuss the causes of failures.

Even with a compressed agenda like that of the WIG sessions, any meeting can run longer than necessary because team members might want to brainstorm about solutions to barriers or might spend too much time trying to identify who is accountable for lack of progress. To keep WIG sessions within ideal time constraints and make them effective tools, the leadership can outline how much time they allotted for each step of the agenda, while understanding that teams new to WIG sessions might require more time. Prior to summarizing at the end of the meeting what each team member will do to advance the WIG measures, a team leader might take a moment to indicate what will be discussed at the next meeting. This kind of "structured close" ensures the meeting wraps up quickly. [6]

Key Takeaway 9

Implementing the four disciplines is a process for the whole team but is driven by the leader. It requires six steps, from clearly defining the WIG and lead measures to training leaders, launching the initiative, constant coaching, and quarterly updates.

Analysis

Implementing the four disciplines in an organization works best when it is established among several teams collaborating together. The first step of the process is defining the WIG. Teams collaborate on the lead measures they will use. The organization trains the team leaders to facilitate the four disciplines in their teams, particularly in directing the scoreboards and weekly WIG sessions. The disciplines are then launched within the teams. As the disciplines are executed, leaders continue to receive coaching in facilitation. Every quarter, the leaders gather in a summit to discuss how the disciplines are working in their teams and whether they have made progress toward the WIG.

When a Navy captain decided to implement the four disciplines of execution on his ship, he chose to roll the program out in phases. The first phase was exploratory to discover the areas where execution was lacking through FranklinCovey's Execution Quotient test. As the captain prepared to announce the focus of the four disciplines, sailors and leaders underwent training and worked under a new code of conduct. The captain announced the execution gaps that would become the three WIGs in phase two, identified the leading indicators for those WIGs by monitoring how top performers in each WIG did their jobs, built scoreboards, and mandated accountability meetings for everyone regardless of rank. The implementation process took a full year, but by the end of the year, the ship had already seen substantial improvements in conduct and retention. [7]

Key Takeaway 10

Common obstacles to implementation can be avoided with consistency, accountability, and focus enforced by the leader.

Analysis

Like any other special initiative, the four disciplines may be abandoned if they are not exercised consistently and if individuals think they will not be held accountable for lack of progress. The key to progress is focusing on the WIG without diverting attention to new goals, keeping the scoreboards updated, and holding regular WIG sessions with accountability. All of these are tasks best directed by leaders.

Mission creep is a danger that embodies the primary obstacles of lack of focus, accountability, and consistency. It is a common problem in new projects where a focused goal with an achievable scope slowly loses that focus as people add extra features and ideas to the project. If no one takes the time to rein in the project's scope or realign the team's energies, the final goal can change entirely and be practically unrecognizable by the time the original goal was intended to be accomplished. A leader's focus can ensure that any tendency toward mission creep is restricted early on and that team members are held accountable for consistently pursuing the narrowly defined goal.

Authors' Style

The 4 Disciplines of Execution is written with a standard business self-help tone of confident instruction and advice. The book's presumed audience is decision-making leaders in the private sector, although some of the examples are in the public sector and a couple of examples show how the disciplines can be applied to raising children or setting family goals.

The authors often refer to surveys conducted by FranklinCovey, but they also rely on anecdotal evidence about asking questions of business leaders during seminars. Sources outside of FranklinCovey are noted in the text and the citations appear at the end of the book divided by chapter.

The book is filled with both examples of companies that implemented the four disciplines and testimonials about their effectiveness from the people who implemented them. The examples and testimonials usually name people and the companies for which they work. On occasion an employer is referred to only by its industry and identifiers, such as its status as a global leader.

Many of the disciplines and their principles are illustrated with diagrams and tables in the text. Often these images are geared toward making the principles memorable.

There is a heavy emphasis on selling the four disciplines to the reader, as well as on FranklinCovey's online

tools, which allow readers to automate some of the prog-
ress-tracking and accountability features. The authors
also spend large portions of the book discussing the process used to create and refine the disciplines. The authors
do not identify scenarios where the four disciplines would
be a poor fit or would not work.

Never is it made clear which author is doing the writ-
ing in a given chapter or to which author a particular
anecdote belongs. Additionally, there are chapters with
significant portions contributed by writers not listed on
the cover.

Authors' Perspective

Chris McChesney, Sean Covey, and Jim Huling are executives at FranklinCovey, an organizational and individual behavior-improvement consultancy created from the merger of the time management business Franklin Quest and the consultancy founded by Sean Covey's father, Stephen Covey. As a result, the authors' work is strongly influenced by the tone, format, and approach of Stephen Covey's classic *The 7 Habits of Highly Effective People* (1989). Huling came to FranklinCovey after implementing the consultancy's programs in the businesses he led.

~~~~ END OF INSTAREAD ~~~~

Thank you for purchasing this Instaread book

**Download the Instaread mobile app to get
unlimited text & audio summaries
of bestselling books.**

Visit Instaread.co
to learn more.

References

1. Grootjans, Nick. "Operational Excellence at Banner." Center for Advanced Research. September 11, 2009. Accessed September 14, 2016. https://www.franklincovey.com/case-study/

2. Keller, Gary, and Jay Papasan. *The One Thing: The Surprisingly Simple Truth Behind Extraordinary Results*. Austin, TX: Bard Press, 2013.

3. Collinwood, Dean. "Progress at a Public Agency." Center for Advanced Research. April 2007. Accessed September 14, 2016. https://www.franklincovey.com/case-study/

4. Korman, Richard. "Dignity Dividend: Civilized Treatment Cuts Accidents." *Engineering News-Record*. April 13, 2016. Accessed September 3, 2016. http://webcache.googleusercontent.com/search?q=cache:BOWixsA146gJ:www.enr.com/articles/39228-dignity-dividend-civilized-treatment-cuts-jobsite-accidents+&cd=1&hl=en&ct=clnk&gl=us

5. Carnegie, Dale. *How to Win Friends and Influence People*. New York: Simon & Schuster, 1936.

6. Daum, Kevin. "3 Ways to Keep Meetings Short (Every Time)." *Inc. Magazine*. September 14, 2012. Accessed September 3, 2016. http://

www.inc.com/kevin-daum/3-ways-to-keep-meetings-short-every-time.html

7. Rose, Hoke. "Unleashing the Talent of a Military Crew." Center for Advanced Research. May 2010. Accessed September 14, 2016. https://www.franklincovey.com/case-study/

Lightning Source UK Ltd.
Milton Keynes UK
UKOW05f1811281216
290947UK00025B/991/P